Arthur Quiller-Couch

Green bays

Arthur Quiller-Couch

Green bays

ISBN/EAN: 9783337733759

Printed in Europe, USA, Canada, Australia, Japan

Cover: Foto ©ninafisch / pixelio.de

More available books at **www.hansebooks.com**

GREEN BAYS

VERSES AND

PARODIES BY

Q

METHUEN AND CO.
18 BURY STREET, W.C.
LONDON
1893

Second Edition

Most of the verses in this volume were written at Oxford, and first appeared in the 'Oxford Magazine.' A few are reprinted from 'The Speaker'; and a few from certain works of fiction published by Messrs. Cassell and Co.   *Q.*

CONTENTS

IN A COLLEGE GARDEN,

THE SPLENDID SPUR,

THE WHITE MOTH,

Irish Melodies—i. TIM THE DRAGOON,

        ii. KENMARE RIVER,

LADY JANE (SAPPHICS),

A TRIOLET,

AN OATH,

UPON GRACIOSA, WALKING AND TALKING,

WRITTEN UPON LOVE'S FRONTIER-POST,

TITANIA,

MEASURE FOR MEASURE,

RETROSPECTION,

WHY THIS VOLUME IS SO THIN,

CONTENTS

Nugae Oxonienses

TWILIGHT,	37
WILLALOO,	39
THE SAIR STROKE,	44
THE DOOM OF THE ESQUIRE BEDELL,	48
'BEHOLD! I AM NOT ONE THAT GOES TO LECTURES,'	51
CALIBAN UPON RUDIMENTS,	54
SOLVITUR ACRIS HIEMPS,	57
A LETTER,	60

Occasional Verses

ANECDOTE FOR FATHERS,	69
UNITY PUT QUARTERLY,	74
FIRE!	77
DE TEA FABULA,	82
L'ENVOI (AS I LAYE A-DREAMYNGE),	86

GREEN BAYS

IN A COLLEGE GARDEN

Senex.   Saye, cushat, callynge from the brake,
    What ayles thee soe to pyne?
  Thy carefulle heart shall cease to ake
    When dayes be fyne
    And greene thynges twyne:
  Saye, cushat, what thy griefe to myne?

Turtur.   Naye, gossyp, loyterynge soe late,
    What ayles thee thus to chyde?
  My love is fled by garden-gate;
    Since Lammas-tyde
    I wayte my bryde.
  Saye, gossyp, whom dost thou abyde?

GREEN BAYS

Senex.   Loe! I am he, the 'Lonelie Manne,'
    Of Time forgotten quite,
  That no remembered face may scanne
      Sadde eremyte,
      I wayte tonyghte
    Pale Death, nor any other wyghte.

O cushat, cushat, callynge lowe,
    Goe waken Time from sleepe :
Goe whysper in his ear, that soe
      His besom sweepe
      Me to that heape
    Where all my recollections keepe.

Hath he forgott?   Or did I viewe
    A ghostlye companye
This even, by the dismalle yewe,
      Of faces three
      That beckoned mee
    To land where no repynynges bee?

IN A COLLEGE GARDEN

O Harrye, Harrye, Tom and Dicke,
   Each lost companion!
Why loyter I among the quicke,
    When ye are gonne?
    Shalle I alone
   Delayinge crye 'Anon, Anon'?

Naye, let the spyder have my gowne,
   To brayde therein her veste.
My cappe shal serve, now I 'goe downe,'
    For mouse's neste.
    Loe! this is best.
   I care not, soe I gayne my reste.

THE SPLENDID SPUR

Not on the neck of prince or hound,
    Nor on a woman's finger twin'd,
May gold from the deriding ground
    Keep sacred that we sacred bind:
        Only the heel
        Of splendid steel
    Shall stand secure on sliding fate,
    When golden navies weep their freight.

The scarlet hat, the laurell'd stave
    Are measures, not the springs, of worth;
In a wife's lap, as in a grave,
    Man's airy notions mix with earth.
        Seek other spur
        Bravely to stir
    The dust in this loud world, and tread
    Alp-high among the whisp'ring dead.

THE SPLENDID SPUR

Trust in thyself,—then spur amain :
So shall Charybdis wear a grace,
Grim Ætna laugh, the Libyan plain
Take roses to her shrivell'd face.
This orb—this round
Of sight and sound—
Count it the lists that God hath built
For haughty hearts to ride a-tilt.

THE WHITE MOTH

If a leaf rustled, she would start :
  And yet she died, a year ago.
How had so frail a thing the heart
  To journey where she trembled so ?
And do they turn and turn in fright,
  Those little feet, in so much night ?

The light above the poet's head
  Streamed on the page and on the cloth,
And twice and thrice there buffeted
  On the black pane a white-wing'd moth :
'Twas Annie's soul that beat outside
  And 'Open, open, open !' cried :

THE WHITE MOTH

'I could not find the way to God;
　There were too many flaming suns
For signposts, and the fearful road
　Led over wastes where millions
Of tangled comets hissed and burned—
　I was bewilder'd and I turned.

'O, it was easy then! I knew
　Your window and no star beside.
Look up, and take me back to you!'
　—He rose and thrust the window wide.
'Twas but because his brain was hot
　With rhyming; for he heard her not.

But poets polishing a phrase
　Show anger over trivial things;
And as she blundered in the blaze
　Towards him, on ecstatic wings,
He raised a hand and smote her dead;
　Then wrote '*That I had died instead!*'

IRISH MELODIES

I

TIM THE DRAGOON

(From 'Troy Town')

Be aisy an' list to a chune
That's sung of bowld Tim the Dragoon—
 Sure, 'twas he'd niver miss
 To be stalin' a kiss,
Or a brace, by the light of the moon—
   Aroon—
Wid a wink at the Man in the Moon!

Rest his sowl where the daisies grow thick;
For he's gone from the land of the quick:
 But he's still makin' love
 To the leddies above,

TIM THE DRAGOON

An' be jabbers! he'll tache 'em the thrick—
    Avick—
Niver doubt but he'll tache 'em the thrick!

'Tis by Tim the dear saints 'll set sthore,
And 'ull thrate him to whisky galore:
   For they've only to sip
   But the tip of his lip
An' bedad! they'll be askin' for more—
    Asthore—
By the powers, they'll be shoutin' 'Ancore!'

IRISH MELODIES

II

KENMARE RIVER

'Tis pretty to be in Ballinderry,
   'Tis pretty to be in Ballindoon,
But 'tis prettier far in County Kerry
   Coortin' under the bran' new moon,
                    Aroon, Aroon!

'Twas there by the bosom of blue Killarney
   They came by the hundther' a-coortin' me;
Sure I was the one to give back their blarney,
   An' merry was I to be fancy-free.

But niver a step in the lot was lighter,
   An' divvle a boulder among the bhoys,
Than Phelim O'Shea, me dynamither,
   Me illigant arthist in clock-work toys.

KENMARE RIVER

'Twas all for love he would bring his figgers
    Of iminent statesmen, in toy machines,
An' hould me hand as he pulled the thriggers
    An' scattered the thraytors to smithereens.

An' to see the Queen in her Crystial Pallus
    Fly up to the roof, an' the windeys broke!
And all with divvle a trace of malus,—
    But he was the bhoy that enjoyed his joke!

Then O, but his cheek would flush, an' 'Bridget,'
    He'd say, 'Will yez love me?' But I'd be coy
And answer him, 'Arrah now, dear, don't fidget!'
    Though at heart I loved him, me arthist bhoy!

One night we stood by the Kenmare river,
    An' 'Bridget, creina, now whist,' said he,
'I'll be goin' to-night, an' may be for iver;
    Open your arms at the last to me.'

GREEN BAYS

'Twas there by the banks of the Kenmare river
    He took in his hands me white, white face,
An' we kissed our first an' our last for iver—
    For Phelim O'Shea is disparsed in space.

'Twas pretty to be by blue Killarney,
    'Twas pretty to hear the linnets's call,
But whist! for I cannot attind their blarney,
    Nor whistle in answer at all, at all.

For the voice that he swore 'ud out-call the linnet's
    Is cracked intoirely, and out of chune,
Since the clock-work missed it by thirteen minutes
    An' scattered me Phelim around the moon,
                    Aroon, Aroon!

LADY JANE

Sapphics

Down the green hill-side fro' the castle window
Lady Jane spied Bill Amaranth a-workin';
Day by day watched him go about his ample
        Nursery garden.

Cabbages thriv'd there, wi' a mort o' green-stuff—
Kidney beans, broad beans, onions, tomatoes,
Artichokes, seakale, vegetable marrows,
        Early potatoes.

Lady Jane cared not very much for all these :
What she cared much for was a glimpse o' Willum
Strippin' his brown arms wi' a view to horti-
        -Cultural effort.

GREEN BAYS

Little guessed Willum, never extra-vain, that
Up the green hill-side, i' the gloomy castle,
Feminine eyes could so delight to view his
                Noble proportions.

Only one day while, in an innocent mood,
Moppin' his brow ('cos 'twas a trifle sweaty)
With a blue kerchief—lo, he spies a white 'un
                Coyly responding.

Oh, delightsome Love! Not a jot do *you* care
For the restrictions set on human inter—
—course by cold-blooded social refiners;
                Nor do I, neither.

Day by day, peepin' fro' behind the bean-sticks,
Willum observed that scrap o' white a-wavin',
Till his hot sighs out-growin' all repression
                Busted his weskit.

LADY JANE

Lady Jane's guardian was a haughty Peer, who
Clung to old creeds and had a nasty temper;
Can we blame Willum that he hardly cared to
      Risk a refusal?

Year by year found him busy 'mid the bean-sticks,
Wholly uncertain how on earth to take steps.
Thus for eighteen years he beheld the maiden
      Wave fro' her window.

But the nineteenth spring, i' the Castle post-bag,
Came by book-post Bill's catalogue o' seedlings
Mark'd wi' blue ink at ' Paragraphs relatin'
      Mainly to Pumpkins.'

'W. A. can,' so the Lady Jane read,
'Strongly commend that very noble Gourd, the
Lady Jane, first-class medal, ornamental;
      Grows to a great height.'

GREEN BAYS

Scarce a year arter, by the scented hedgerows—
Down the mown hill-side, fro' the castle gateway—
Came a long train and, i' the midst, a black bier,
> Easily shouldered.

'Whose is yon corse that, thus adorned wi' gourd-
> leaves,
Forth ye bear with slow step?' A mourner answer'd,
''Tis the poor clay-cold body Lady Jane grew
> Tired to abide in.'

'Delve my grave quick, then, for I die to-morrow.
Delve it one furlong fro' the kidney bean-sticks,
Where I may dream she's goin' on precisely
> As she was used to.'

Hardly died Bill when, fro' the Lady Jane's grave,
Crept to his white death-bed a lovely pumpkin:
Climb'd the house wall and over-arched his head wi'
> Billowy verdure.

LADY JANE

Simple this tale!—but delicately perfumed
As the sweet roadside honeysuckle.   That's why,
Difficult though its metre was to tackle,
                    I'm glad I wrote it.

A TRIOLET

To commemorate the virtue of Homœopathy in restoring one apparently drowned

Love, that in a tear was drown'd,
Lives revivéd by a tear.
Stella heard them mourn around
Love that in a tear was drown'd,
Came and coax'd his dripping swound,
Wept *'The fault was mine, my dear!'*
Love, that in a tear was drown'd,
Lives, revivéd by a tear.

AN OATH

(From 'Troy Town')

A MONTH ago Lysander pray'd
    To Jove, to Cupid, and to Venus,
That he might die if he betray'd
    A single vow that pass'd between us.

Ah, careless gods, to hear so ill
    And cheat a maid on you relying!
For false Lysander's thriving still,
    And 'tis Corinna lies a-dying.

UPON GRACIOSA, WALKING AND TALKING

(From 'Troy Town')

When as abroad, to greet the morn,
I mark my Graciosa walk,
In homage bends the whisp'ring corn,
      Yet to confess
      Its awkwardness
Must hang its head upon the stalk.

And when she talks, her lips do heal
The wounds her lightest glances give :—
In pity then be harsh, and deal
      Such wounds that I
      May hourly die,
And, by a word restoréd, live.

LOVE'S FRONTIER-POST

WRITTEN
UPON
LOVE'S FRONTIER-POST

(From 'Troy Town')

Toiling lover, loose your pack,
    All your sighs and tears unbind:
Care's a ware will break a back,
    Will not bend a maiden's mind.

In this State a man shall need
    Neither priest nor law giver:
Those same lips that are his creed
    Shall confess their worshipper.

All the laws he must obey,
    Now in force and now repeal'd,
Shift in eyes that shift as they,
    Till alike with kisses seal'd.

TITANIA

By Lord T——n

So bluff Sir Leolin gave the bride away :
And when they married her, the little church
Had seldom seen a costlier ritual.
The coach and pair alone were two-pound-ten,
And two-pound-ten apiece the wedding-cakes;—
Three wedding-cakes. A Cupid poised a-top
Of each hung shivering to the frosted loves
Of two fond cushats on a field of ice,
As who should say '*I* see you !'—Such the joy
When English-hearted Edwin swore his faith
With Mariana of the Moated Grange.

For Edwin, plump head-waiter at The Cock,
Grown sick of custom, spoilt of plenitude,
Lacking the finer wit that saith, 'I wait,
They come ; and if I make them wait, they go,'

TITANIA

Fell in a jaundiced humour petulant-green,
Watched the dull clerk slow-rounding to his cheese,
Flicked a full dozen flies that flecked the pane—
All crystal-cheated of the fuller air,
Blurted a free 'Good-day t' ye,' left and right,
And shaped his gathering choler to this head :—

'Custom! And yet what profit of it all?
The old order changeth yielding place to new,
To me small change, and this the Counter-change
Of custom beating on the self-same bar—
Change out of chop. Ah me! the talk, the tip,
The would-be-evening should-be-mourning suit,
The forged solicitude for petty wants
More petty still than they,—all these I loathe,
Learning they lie who feign that all things come
To him that waiteth. I have waited long,
And now I go, to mate me with a bride
Who is aweary waiting, even as I!'

But when the amorous moon of honeycomb
Was over, ere the matron-flower of Love—
Step-sister of To-morrow's marmalade—
Swooned scentless, Mariana found her lord
Did something jar the nicer feminine sense
With usage, being all too fine and large,
Instinct of warmth and colour, with a trick
Of blunting 'Mariana's' keener edge
To 'Mary Ann'—the same but not the same:
Whereat she girded, tore her crispéd hair,
Called him 'Sir Churl,' and ever calling 'Churl!'
Drave him to Science, then to Alcohol,
To forge a thousand theories of the rocks,
Then somewhat else for thousands dewy cool,
Wherewith he sought a more Pacific isle
And there found love, a duskier love than hers.

MEASURE FOR MEASURE

By O——r K——m

Wake! for the closed Pavilion doors have kept
Their silence while the white-eyed Kaffir slept,
  And wailed the Nightingale with 'Jug, jug, jug!'
Whereat, for empty cup, the White Rose wept.

Enter with me where yonder door hangs out
Its Red Triangle to a world of drought,
  Inviting to the Palace of the Djinn,
Where Death, Aladdin, waits as Chuckeroût.

Methought, last night, that one in suit of woe
Stood by the Tavern-door and whispered, 'Lo,
  The Pledge departed, what avails the Cup?
Then take the Pledge and let the Wine-cup go.'

But I : 'For every thirsty soul that drains
This Anodyne of Thought its rim contains—
   Free-will the *can,* Necessity the *must,*
Pour off the *must,* and, see, the *can* remains.

'Then, pot or glass, why label it " *With Care* " ?
Or why your Sheepskin with my Gourd compare ?
   Lo ! here the Bar and I the only Judge :—
O, Dog that bit me, I exact an hair !'

We are the Sum of things, who jot our score
With Cæsar's clay behind the Tavern door :
   And Alexander's armies—where are they,
But gone to Pot—that Pot you push for more ?

And this same Jug I empty, could it speak,
Might whisper that itself had been a Beak
   And dealt me Fourteen Days ' without the Op.'—
Your Worship, see, my lip is on your cheek.

MEASURE FOR MEASURE

Yourself condemned to three score years and ten,
Say, did you judge the ways of other men?
   Why, now, sir, you are hourly filled with wine,
And has the clay more licence now than then?

Life is a draught, good sir; its brevity
Gives you and me our measures, and thereby
   Has docked your virtue to a tankard's span,
And left of my criterion—a Cri'!

RETROSPECTION

After C. S. C.

When the hunter-star Orion
    (Or, it may be, Charles his Wain)
Tempts the tiny elves to try on
    All their little tricks again;
When the earth is calmly breathing
    Draughts of slumber undefiled,
And the sire, unused to teething,
    Seeks for errant pins his child;

When the moon is on the ocean,
    And our little sons and heirs
From a natural emotion
    Wish the luminary theirs;

RETROSPECTION

Then a feeling hard to stifle,
   Even harder to define,
Makes me feel I 'd give a trifle
   For the days of Auld Lang Syne.

James—for we have been as brothers
   (Are, to speak correctly, twins),
Went about in one another's
   Clothing, bore each other's sins,
Rose together, ere the pearly
   Tint of morn had left the heaven,
And retired (absurdly early)
   Simultaneously at seven—

James, the days of yore were pleasant.
   Sweet to climb for alien pears
Till the irritated peasant
   Came and took us unawares;

GREEN BAYS

Sweet to devastate his chickens,
    As the ambush'd catapult
Scattered, and the very dickens
    Was the natural result;

Sweet to snare the thoughtless rabbit;
    Break the next-door neighbour's pane;
Cultivate the smoker's habit
    On the not-innocuous cane;
Leave the exercise unwritten;
    Systematically cut
Morning school, to plunge the kitten
    In his bath, the water-butt.

Age, my James, that from the cheek of
    Beauty steals its rosy hue,
Has not left us much to speak of:
    But 'tis not for this I rue.

RETROSPECTION

Beauty with its thousand graces,
    Hair and tints that will not fade,
You may get from many places
    Practically ready-made.

No ; it is the evanescence
    Of those lovelier tints of Hope—
Bubbles, such as adolescence
    Joys to win from melted soap—
Emphasizing the conclusion
    That the dreams of Youth remain
Castles that are An delusion
    (Castles, that's to say, in Spain).

Age thinks 'fit,' and I say 'fiat.'
    Here I stand for Fortune's butt
As for Sunday swains to shy at
    Stands the stoic coco-nut.

GREEN BAYS

If you wish it put succinctly,
    Gone are all our little games;
But I thought I'd say distinctly
    What I feel about it, James.

WHY THIS VOLUME IS SO THIN

In youth I dreamed, as other youths have dreamt,
  Of love, and thrummed an amateur guitar
To verses of my own,—a stout attempt
  To hold communion with the Evening Star
I wrote a sonnet, rhymed it, made it scan.
Ah me! how trippingly those last lines ran.—

O Hesperus! O happy star! to bend
  O'er Helen's bosom in the trancéd west,
  To watch the hours heave by upon her breast,
And at her parted lip for dreams attend—
  If dawn defraud thee, how shall I be deemed,
  Who house within that bosom, and am dreamed?

For weeks I thought these lines remarkable;
   For weeks I put on airs and called myself
A bard: till on a day, as it befell,
   I took a small green Moxon from the shelf
At random, opened at a casual place,
And found my young illusions face to face

With this:—'*Still steadfast, still unchangeable,*
   Pillow'd upon my fair Love's ripening breast
To feel for ever its soft fall and swell,
   Awake for ever in a sweet unrest;
Still, still to hear her tender-taken breath,
And so live ever,—or else swoon to death.'

O gulf not to be crossed by taking thought!
   O heights by toil not to be overcome!
Great Keats, unto your altar straight I brought
   My speech, and from the shrine departed dumb.
—And yet sometimes I think you played it hard
Upon a rather hopeful minor bard.

NUGAE OXONIENSES

TWILIGHT

By W—ll—m C—wp—r

'Tis evening.   See with its resorting throng
Rude Carfax teems, and waistcoats, visited
With too-familiar elbow, swell the curse
Vortiginous.   The boating man returns,
His rawness growing with experience—
Strange union! and directs the optic glass
Not unresponsive to Jemima's charms,
Who wheels obdurate, in his mimic chaise
Perambulant, the child.   The gouty cit,
Asthmatical, with elevated cane
Pursues the unregarding tram, as one
Who, having heard a hurdy-gurdy, girds
His loins and hunts the hurdy-gurdy-man,
Blaspheming.   Now the clangorous bell proclaims

GREEN BAYS

The *Times* or *Chronicle,* and Rauca screams
The latest horrid murder in the ear
Of nervous dons expectant of the urn
And mild domestic muffin.
      To the Parks
Drags the slow Ladies' School, consuming time
In passing given points. Here glow the lamps,
And tea-spoons clatter to the cosy hum
Of scientific circles. Here resounds
The football-field with its discordant train,
The crowd that cheers but not discriminates,
As ever into touch the ball returns
And shrieks the whistle, while the game proceeds
With fine irregularity well worth
The paltry shilling.—
      Draw the curtains close
While I resume the night-cap dear to all
Familiar with my illustrated works.

WILLALOO

By E. A. P.

In the sad and sodden street,
> To and fro,

Flit the fever-stricken feet

Of the freshers as they meet,
> Come and go,

Ever buying, buying, buying

Where the shopmen stand supplying,
> Vying, vying
> All they know,

While the Autumn lies a-dying
> Sad and low

As the price of summer suitings when the winter breezes blow,

GREEN BAYS

Of the summer, summer suitings that are standing in
    a row
On the way to Jericho.

    See the freshers as they row
        To and fro,
Up and down the Lower River for an afternoon or
        so—
    (For the deft manipulation
        Of the never-resting oar,
    Though it lead to approbation,
    Will induce excoriation)—
    They are infinitely sore,
        Keeping time, time, time
        In a sort of Runic rhyme
Up and down the way to Iffley in an afternoon or so :
        (Which is slow).
        Do they blow ?

WILLALOO

'Tis the wind and nothing more,
'Tis the wind that in Vacation has a tendency to go:
But the coach's objurgation and his tendency to
'score'
Will be sated—nevermore.

See the freshers in the street,
    The *élite*!
Their apparel how unquestionably neat!
How delighted at a distance,
    Inexpensively attired,
I have wondered with persistence
At their butterfly existence!
    How admired!
And the payment—O, the payment!
It is tardy for the raiment:
Yet the haberdasher gloats as he sells,
    And he tells,

GREEN BAYS

'This is best
To be dress'd
Rather better than the rest,
To be noticeably drest,
To be swells,
To be swells, swells, swells, swells,
Swells, swells, swells,
To be simply and indisputably swells.'

See the freshers one or two,
Just a few,
Now on view,
Who are sensibly and innocently new;
How they cluster, cluster, cluster
Round the rugged walls of Worcester!
See them stand,
Book in hand,
In the garden ground of John's!
How they dote upon their Dons!

WILLALOO

See in every man a Blue!

It is true

They are lamentably few;

But I spied

Yesternight upon the staircase just a pair of boots outside

Upon the floor,

Just a little pair of boots upon the stairs where I reside,

Lying there and nothing more;

And I swore

While these dainty twins continued sentry by the chamber door

That the hope their presence planted should be with me evermore,

Should desert me—nevermore.

THE SAIR STROKE

O waly, waly, my bonnie crew
　　Gin ye maun bumpit be!
And waly, waly, my Stroke sae true,
　　Ye leuk unpleasauntlie!

O hae ye suppit the sad sherrie
　　That gars the wind gae soon;
Or hae ye pu'd o' the braw bird's e'e,
　　Ye be sae stricken doun?

I hae na suppit the sad sherrie,
　　For a' my heart is sair;
For Keiller's still i' the bonnie Dundee,
　　And his is halesome fare.

THE SAIR STROKE

But I hae slain our gude Captain,
   That c'uld baith shout and sweer,
And ither twain put out o' pain—
   The Scribe and Treasurere.

There's ane lies stark by the meadow-gate
   And twa by the black, black brig:
And waefu', waefu', was the fate
   That gar'd them there to lig!

They waked us soon, they warked us lang,
   Wearily did we greet;
'*Should he abrade*' was a' our sang,
   Our food but butcher's-meat.

We hadna train'd but ower a week,
   A week, but barely twa,
Three sonsie steeds they fared to seek,
   That mightna gar them fa'.

GREEN BAYS

They 've ta'en us ower the lang, lang coorse,
    And wow! but it was wark;
And ilka coach he sware him hoorse,
    That ilka man s'uld hark.

Then upped and spake our pawkie bow,
    —O, but he wasna late!
'Now who shall gar them cry *Enow*,
    That gang this fearsome gate?'

Syne he has ta'en his boatin' cap,
    And cast the keevils in,
And wha but me to gae (God hap!)
    And stay our Captain's din?

I stayed his din by the meadow-gate,
    His feres' by Nnneham brig,
And waefu', waefu', was the fate
    That gar'd them there to lig!

THE SAIR STROKE

O, waly to the welkin's top!
    And waly round the braes!
And waly all about the shop
    (To use a Southron phrase).

Rede ither crews be debonair,
    But we've a weird to dree,
I wis we maun be bumpit sair
    By boaties two and three:
Sing stretchers of yew for our Toggere,
    Sith we maun bumpit be!

GREEN BAYS

THE DOOM OF THE ESQUIRE BEDELL

    Adown the torturing mile of street
        I mark him come and go,
    Thread in and out with tireless feet
        The crossings to and fro;
    A soul that treads without retreat
        A labyrinth of woe.

    Palsied with awe of such despair,
        All living things give room,
    They flit before his sightless glare
        As horrid shapes, that loom
    And shriek the curse that bids him bear
        The symbol of his doom.

THE DOOM OF THE ESQUIRE BEDELL

The very stones are coals that bake
    And scorch his fevered skin;
A fire no hissing hail may slake
    Consumes his heart within.
Still must he hasten on to rake
    The furnace of his sin.

Still forward! forward! For he feels
    Fierce claws that pluck his breast,
And blindly beckon as he reels
    Upon his awful quest:
For there is that behind his heels
    Knows neither ruth nor rest.

The fiends in hell have flung the dice;
    The destinies depend
On feet that run for fearful price,
    And fangs that gape to rend;

GREEN BAYS

And still the footsteps of his Vice

Pursue him to the end :—

The feet of his incarnate Vice

Shall dog him to the end.

'BEHOLD! I AM NOT ONE THAT GOES...'

'BEHOLD! I AM NOT ONE THAT GOES TO LECTURES'

By W. W.

BEHOLD! I am not one that goes to Lectures or the
pow-wow of Professors.
The elementary laws never apologise: neither do
I apologise.
I find letters from the Dean dropt on my table—and
every one is signed by the Dean's name—
And I leave them where they are; for I know that
as long as I stay up
Others will punctually come for ever and ever.
I am one who goes to the river,
I sit in the boat and think of 'life' and of
'time.'

How life is much, but time is more ; and the beginning is everything,

But the end is something.

I loll in the Parks, I go to the wicket, I swipe.

I see twenty-two young men from Foster's watching me, and the trousers of the twenty-two young men,

I see the Balliol men *en masse* watching me.—The Hottentot that loves his mother, the untutored Bedowee, the Cave-man that wears only his certificate of baptism, and the shaggy Sioux that hangs his testamur with his scalps.

I see the Don who ploughed me in Rudiments watching me: and the wife of the Don who ploughed me in Rudiments watching me.

I see the rapport of the wicket-keeper and umpire.

I cannot see that I am out.

Oh ! you Umpires !

'BEHOLD! I AM NOT ONE THAT GOES . . .'

I am not one who greatly cares for experience, soap, bull-dogs, cautions, majorities, or a graduated Income-Tax,
The certainty of space, punctuation, sexes, institutions, copiousness, degrees, committees, delicatesse, or the fetters of rhyme—
For none of these do I care: but least for the fetters of rhyme.
Myself only I sing. Me Imperturbe! Me Prononcé!
Me progressive and the depth of me progressive,
And the βάθος, *Anglicé* bathos
Of me chanting to the Public the song of Simple Enumeration.

CALIBAN UPON RUDIMENTS[1]

OR

AUTOSCHEDIASTIC THEOLOGY IN A HOLE

RUDIMENTS, Rudiments, and Rudiments!
'Thinketh one made them i' the fit o' the blues.

'Thinketh one made them with the 'tips' to match,
But not the answers; 'doubteth there be none,
Only Guides, Helps, Analyses, such as that:
Also this Beast, that groweth sleek thereon,
And snow-white bands that round the neck o' the same.

'Thinketh, it came of being ill at ease.
'Hath heard that Satan finds some mischief still
For idle hands, and the rest o't. That's the case.

[1] Caliban museth of the now extinct Examination in the Rudiments of Faith and Religion.

CALIBAN UPON RUDIMENTS

Also 'hath heard they pop the names i' the hat,
Toss out a brace, a dozen stick inside;
Let forty through and plough the sorry rest.

'Thinketh, such shows nor right nor wrong in them,
Only their strength, being made o' sloth i' the main—
'Am strong myself compared to yonder names
O' Jewish towns i' the paper. Watch th' event—
'Let twenty pass, 'have a shot at twenty-first,
'Miss Ramoth-Gilead, 'take Jehoiakim,
'Let Abner by and spot Melchizedek,
Knowing not, caring not, just choosing so,
As it likes me each time, I do: so they.

'Saith they be terrible: watch their feats i' the Viva!
One question plays the deuce with six months' toil.
Aha, if they would tell me! No, not they!
There is the sport: ' come read me right or die!'

GREEN BAYS

All at their mercy,—why they like it most

When—when—well, never try the same shot twice!

'Hath fled himself and only got up a tree.

    .   •   •   ,   •   •

'Will say a plain word if he gets a plough.

SOLVITUR ACRIS HIEMPS

My Juggins, see: the pasture green,
  Obeying Nature's kindly law,
Renews its mantle; there has been
    A thaw.

The frost-bound earth is free at last,
  That lay 'neath Winter's sullen yoke
'Till people felt it getting past
    A joke.

Now forth again the Freshers fare,
  And get them tasty summer suits
Wherein they flaunt afield and scare
    The brutes.

GREEN BAYS

Again the stream suspects the keel;
    Again the shrieking captain drops
Upon his crew; again the meal
        Of chops

Divides the too-laborious day;
    Again the Student sighs o'er Mods,
And prompts his enemies to lay
        Long odds.

Again the shopman spreads his wiles;
    Again the organ-pipes, unbound,
Distract the populace for miles
        Around.

Then, Juggins, ere December's touch
    Once more the wealth of Spring reclaim,
Since each successive year is much
        The same;

SOLVITUR ACRIS HIEMPS

Since too the monarch on his throne
    In purple lapped and frankincense,
Who from his infancy has blown
        Expense,

No less than he who barely gets
    The boon of out-of-door relief,
Must see desuetude,—come let's
        Be brief.

At those resolves last New Year's Day
    The easy gods indulgent wink.
Then downward, ho!—the shortest way
        Is drink.

GREEN BAYS

A LETTER

Addressed during the Summer Term of 1888 *by* MR. ALGERNON DEXTER, *Scholar of* —— *College, Oxford, to his cousin,* MISS KITTY TREMAYNE, *at* —— *Vicarage, Devonshire.*

AFTER W. M. P.

DEAR KITTY,
    At length the term's ending;
  I'm in for my Schools in a week;
And the time that at present I'm spending
  On you should be spent upon Greek:
But I'm fairly well read in my Plato,
  I'm thoroughly red in the eyes,
And I've almost forgotten the way to
  Be healthy and wealthy and wise.
So 'the best of all ways'—why repeat you
  The verse at 2.30 a.m.,
When I'm stealing an hour to entreat you
  Dear Kitty, to come to Commem.?

A LETTER

Oh, come! You shall rustle in satin
  Through halls where Examiners trod:
Your laughter shall triumph o'er Latin
  In lecture-room, garden, and quad.
They stand in the silent Sheldonian—
  Our orators, waiting—for you,
Their style guaranteed Ciceronian,
  Their subject—'the Ladies in Blue.'
The Vice sits arrayed in his scarlet;
  He's pale, but they say he dissem-
-bles by calling his Beadle a 'varlet'
  Whenever he thinks of Commem.

There are dances, flirtations at Nuneham,
  Flower-shows, the procession of Eights:
There's a list stretching *usque ad Lunam*
  Of concerts, and lunches, and fêtes:
There's the Newdigate all about 'Gordon,
  —So sweet, and they say it will scan.

You shall flirt with a Proctor, a Warden
    Shall run for your shawl and your fan.
They are sportive as gods broken loose from
    Olympus, and yet very em-
-inent men. There are plenty to choose from,
    You'll find, if you come to Commem.

I know your excuses: Red Sorrel
    Has stumbled and broken her knees;
Aunt Phœbe thinks waltzing immoral;
    And 'Algy, you are such a tease;
It's nonsense, of course, but she *is* strict';
    And little Dick Hodge has the croup;
And there's no one to visit your 'district'
    Or make Mother Tettleby's soup.
Let them cease for a se'nnight to plague you;
    Oh, leave them to manage *pro tem*.
With their croups and their soups and their ague,
    Dear Kitty, and come to Commem.

A LETTER

Don't tell me Papa has lumbago,
    That you haven't a frock fit to wear,
That the curate 'has notions, and may go
    To lengths if there's nobody there,'
That the Squire has 'said things' to the Vicar,
    And the Vicar 'had words' with the Squire,
That the Organist's taken to liquor,
    And leaves you to manage the choir:
For Papa must be cured, and the curate
    Coerced, and your gown is a gem;
And the moral is—Don't be obdurate,
    Dear Kitty, but come to Commem.

'My gown? Though, no doubt, sir, you're clever,
    You'd better leave fashions alone.
Do you think that a frock lasts for ever?'
    Dear Kitty, I'll grant you have grown;
But I thought of my 'scene' with McVittie
    That night when he trod on your train

GREEN BAYS

At the Bachelor's Ball. ' 'Twas a pity,'
    You said, but I knew 'twas Champagne.
And your gown was enough to compel me
    To fall down and worship its hem—
(Are 'hems' wearing? If not, you shall tell me
    What is, when you come to Commem.)

Have you thought, since that night, of the Grotto?
    Of the words whispered under the palms,
While the minutes flew by and forgot to
    Remind us of Aunt and her qualms?
Of the stains of the old *Journalisten?*
    Of the rose that I begged from your hair?
When you turned, and I saw something glisten—
    Dear Kitty, don't frown; it *was* there!
But that idiot Delane in the middle
    Bounced in with 'Our dance, I—ahem!'
And—the rose you may find in my Liddell
    And Scott when you come to Commem.

OCCASIONAL VERSES

ANECDOTE FOR FATHERS

Designed to show that the practice of lying is not confined to children

By the late W. W. (of H.M. Inland Revenue Service)

AND is it so? Can Folly stalk
And aim her unrespecting darts
In shades where grave Professors walk
   And Bachelors of Arts?

I have a boy, not six years old,
A sprite of birth and lineage high
His birth I did myself behold,
   His caste is in his eye.

And oh! his limbs are full of grace,
His boyish beauty past compare:
His mother's joy to wash his face,
   And mine to brush his hair!

GREEN BAYS

One morn we strolled on our short walk,
With four goloshes on our shoes,
And held the customary talk
  That parents love to use.

(And oft I turn it into verse,
And write it down upon a page,
Which, being sold, supplies my purse
  And ministers to age.)

So as we paced the curving High,
To view the sights of Oxford town
We raised our feet (like Nelly Bly),
  And then we put them down.

'Now, little Edward, answer me'—
I said, and clutched him by the gown—
'At Cambridge would you rather be,
  Or here in Oxford town?'

ANECDOTE FOR FATHERS

My boy replied with tiny frown
(He'd been a year at Cavendish),
'I'd rather dwell in Oxford town,
   If I could have my wish.'

'Now, little Edward, say why so;
My little Edward, tell me why.'
'Well, really, Pa, I hardly know.'
   'Remarkable!' said I :

'For Cambridge has her "King's Parade,"
And much the more becoming gown ;
Why should you slight her so,' I said,
   'Compared with Oxford town ?'

At this my boy hung down his head,
While sterner grew the parent's eye ;
And six-and-thirty times I said,
   'Come, Edward, tell me why ?'

GREEN BAYS

For I loved Cambridge (where they deal—
How strange!—in butter by the yard);
And so, with every third appeal,
    I hit him rather hard.

Twelve times I struck, as may be seen
(For three times twelve is thirty-six),
When in a shop the *Magazine*
    His tearful sight did fix.

He saw it plain, it made him smile,
And thus to me he made reply :—
'*At Oxford there's a Crocodile;* [1]
    And that's the reason why.'

---

[1] Certain obscure paragraphs relating to a crocodile, kept at the Museum, had been perplexing the readers of the *Oxford Magazine* for some time past, and had been distorted into an allegory of portentous meaning.

ANECDOTE FOR FATHERS

Oh, Mr. Editor! my heart
For deeper lore would seldom yearn,
Could I believe the hundredth part
  Of what from you I learn.

UNITY PUT QUARTERLY[1]

By A. C. S.

THE Centuries kiss and commingle,
Cling, clasp, and are knit in a chain;
No cycle but scorns to be single,
No two but demur to be twain,
'Till the land of the lute and the love-tale
Be bride of the boreal breast,
And the dawn with the darkness shall dovetail,
    The East with the West.

The desire of the grey for the dun nights
Is that of the dun for the grey;
The tales of the Thousand and One Nights
Touch lips with 'The Times' of to-day.—

[1] Suggested by an Article in the *Quarterly Review*, enforcing the unity of literature ancient and modern, and the necessity of providing a new School of Literature in Oxford.

UNITY PUT QUARTERLY

Come, chasten the cheap with the classic;
Choose, Churton, thy chair and thy class,
Mix, melt in the must that is Massic
    The beer that is Bass!

Omnipotent age of the Aorist!
Infinitely freely exact!—
As the fragrance of fiction is fairest
If frayed in the furnace of fact—
Though nine be the Muses in number
There is hope if the handbook be one,—
Dispelling the planets that cumber
    The path of the sun.

Though crimson thy hands and thy hood be
With the blood of a brother betrayed,
O Would-be-Professor of Would-be,
We call thee to bless and to aid.

GREEN BAYS

Transmuted would travel with Er, see
The Land of the Rolling of Logs,
Charmed, chained to thy side, as to Circe
  The Ithacan hogs.

O bourne of the black and the godly!
O land where the good niggers go.
With the books that are borrowed of Bodley,
Old moons and our castaway clo'!
There, there, till the roses be ripened
Rebuke us, revile, and review,
Then take thee thine annual stipend
  So long over-due.

FIRE !

By Sir W. S.

Written on the occasion of the visit of the United Fire Brigades to Oxford, 1887

I

St. Giles's street is fair and wide,
   St. Giles's street is long;
But long or wide, may naught abide
   Therein of guile or wrong;
For through St. Giles's, to and fro,
The mild ecclesiastics go
   From prime to evensong.
It were a fearsome task, perdie!
To sin in such good company.

II

Long had the slanting beam of day
Proclaimed the Thirtieth of May
Ere now, erect, its fiery heat
Illumined all that hallowed street,
And breathing benediction on
Thy serried battlements, St. John,
Suffused at once with equal glow
The cluster'd Archipelago,
The Art Professor's studio
   And Mr. Greenwood's shop,
Thy building, Pusey, where below
The stout Salvation soldiers blow
   The cornet till they drop;
Thine, Balliol, where we move, and oh!
   Thine, Randolph, where we stop.

FIRE!

III

But what is this that frights the air,
And wakes the curate from his lair
   In Pusey's cool retreat,
To leave the feast, to climb the stair,
   And scan the startled street?
As when perambulate the young
And call with unrelenting tongue
   On home, mamma, and sire;
Or voters shout with strength of lung
   For Hall & Co's Entire;
Or Sabbath-breakers scream and shout—
The band of Booth, with drum devout,
Eliza on her Sunday out,
   Or Farmer with his choir :—

IV

E'en so, with shriek of fife and drum
 And horrid clang of brass,
The Fire Brigades of England come
 And down St. Giles's pass.
Oh grand, methinks, in such array
To spend a Whitsun Holiday
 All soaking to the skin!
(Yet shoes and hose alike are stout;
The shoes to keep the water out,
 The hose to keep it in.)

V

They came from Henley on the Thames,
 From Berwick on the Tweed,
And at the mercy of the flames
They left their children and their dames,

FIRE !

To come and play their little games
    On Morrell's dewy mead.
Yet feared they not with fire to play—
The pyrotechnics (so they say)
    Were very fine indeed.

VI

(P.S. BY LORD MACAULAY)

Then let us bless Our Gracious Queen and eke the Fire Brigade,
And bless no less the horrid mess they've been and gone and made;
Remove the dirt they chose to squirt upon our best attire,
Bless all, but most the lucky chance that no one shouted 'Fire!'

DE TEA FABULA

PLAIN LANGUAGE FROM TRUTHFUL JAMES[1]

> Do I sleep? Do I dream?
>   Am I hoaxed by a scout?
> Are things what they seem,
>   Or is Sophists about?
> Is our τὸ τί ἦν εἶναι a failure, or is Robert Browning played out?
>
>   Which expressions like these
>   May be fairly applied
>   By a party who sees
>   A Society skied
> Upon tea that the Warden of Keble had biled with legitimate pride.

[1] The Oxford Browning Society expired at Keble the week before this was written.

DE TEA FABULA

'Twas November the third,
And I says to Bill Nye,
'Which it's true what I've heard:
If you're, so to speak, fly,
There's a chance of some tea and cheap culture, the sort recommended as High.'

Which I mentioned its name,
And he ups and remarks:
'If dress-coats is the game
And pow-wow in the Parks,
Then I'm nuts on Sordello and Hohenstiel-Schwangau and similar Snarks.'

Now the pride of Bill Nye
Cannot well be express'd;
For he wore a white tie
And a cut-away vest:
Says I, 'Solomon's lilies ain't in it, and they was reputed well dress'd.'

GREEN BAYS

> But not far did we wend,
> > When we saw Pippa pass
> > On the arm of a friend
> > > —Doctor Furnivall 'twas,
> And he wore in his hat two half-tickets for London, return, second-class.

> > 'Well,' I thought, 'this is odd.'
> > > But we came pretty quick
> > > To a sort of a quad
> > > > That was all of red brick,
> And I says to the porter,—' R. Browning : free passes ; and kindly look slick.'

> > But says he, dripping tears
> > > In his check handkerchief,
> > 'That symposium's career's
> > > Been regrettably brief,
> For it went all its pile upon crumpets and busted on gunpowder-leaf!'

DE TEA FABULA

Then we tucked up the sleeves
    Of our shirts (that were biled),
Which the reader perceives
    That our feelings were riled,
And we went for that man till his mother had doubted the traits of her child.

Which emotions like these
    Must be freely indulged
By a party who sees
    A Society bulged
On a reef the existence of which its prospectus had never divulged.

But I ask,—Do I dream?
    Has it gone up the spout?
Are things what they seem,
    Or is Sophists about?
Is our τὸ τί ἦν εἶναι a failure, or is Robert Browning played out?

L'ENVOI

AS I LAYE A-DREAMYNGE

After T. I.

As I laye a-dreamynge, a-dreamynge, a-dreamynge,
O softlye moaned the dove to her mate within the tree,
    And meseemed unto my syghte
    Came rydynge many a knyghte
    All cased in armoure bryghte
        Cap-à-pie,
As I laye a-dreamynge, a goodlye companye!

As I laye a-dreamynge, a-dreamynge, a-dreamynge,
O sadlye mourned the dove, callynge long and callynge lowe,

L'ENVOI

And meseemed of alle that hoste
Notte a face but was the ghoste
Of a friend that I hadde loste
    Long agoe.
As I laye a-dreamynge, oh, bysson teare to flowe!

As I laye a-dreamynge, a-dreamynge, a-dreamynge,
O sadlye sobbed the dove as she seeméd to despayre,
    And laste upon the tracke
    Came one I hayled as 'Jacke!'
    But he turnéd mee his backe
    With a stare:
As I laye a-dreamynge, he lefte mee callynge there.

Stille I laye a-dreamynge, a-dreamynge, a-dreamynge,
And gentler sobbed the dove as it eased her of her payne,

GREEN BAYS

And meseemed a voyce yt cry'd—
'They shall ryde, and they shall ryde
'Tyll the truce of tyme and tyde
    Come agayne!
Alle for Eldorado, yette never maye attayne!'

Stille I laye a-dreamynge, a-dreamynge, a-dreamynge,
And scarcelye moaned the dove, as her agonye was spente:
'Shalle to-morrowe see them nygher
To a golden walle or spyre?
You have better in yr fyre,
    Bee contente.'
As I laye a-dreamynge, it seem'd smalle punyshment.

But I laye a-wakynge, and loe! the dawne was breakynge
And rarely pyped a larke for the promyse of the daye:

L'ENVOI

'Uppe and sette y^r lance in reste!
Uppe and followe on the queste!
Leave the issue to be guessed
    At the endynge of the waye'—

As I laye a-wakynge, 'twas soe she seemed to say—
    'Whatte and if it alle be feynynge?
    There be better thynges than gaynynge,
    Rycher pryzes than attaynynge.'—
    And 'twas truthe she seemed to saye
Whyles the dawne was breakynge, I rode upon my waye.

THE END

EDINBURGH: T. and A. CONSTABLE
Printers to Her Majesty

A LIST OF NEW BOOKS AND ANNOUNCEMENTS OF METHUEN AND COMPANY PUBLISHERS : LONDON 18 BURY STREET W.C.

CONTENTS

	PAGE
FORTHCOMING BOOKS,	2
POETRY,	6
HISTORY AND BIOGRAPHY,	7
GENERAL LITERATURE,	8
WORKS BY S. BARING GOULD,	9
FICTION,	10
NOVEL SERIES,	11
BOOKS FOR BOYS AND GIRLS,	12
ENGLISH LEADERS OF RELIGION,	13
UNIVERSITY EXTENSION SERIES,	14
SOCIAL QUESTIONS OF TO-DAY,	15

OCTOBER 1892

OCTOBER 1892.

MESSRS. METHUEN'S
AUTUMN ANNOUNCEMENTS

GENERAL LITERATURE

Rudyard Kipling. BARRACK-ROOM BALLADS; And Other Verses. By RUDYARD KIPLING. *Extra Post 8vo, pp.* 208. *Laid paper, rough edges, buckram, gilt top.* 6s.

A special Presentation Edition, *bound in white buckram, with extra gilt ornament.* 7s. 6d.

The First Edition was sold on publication, and two further large Editions have been exhausted. The Fourth Edition is Now Ready.

Gladstone. THE SPEECHES AND PUBLIC ADDRESSES OF THE RT. HON. W. E. GLADSTONE, M.P. With Notes. Edited by A. W. HUTTON, M.A. (Librarian of the Gladstone Library), and H. J. COHEN, M.A. With Portraits. 8vo. *Vol. IX.* 12s. 6d.

Messrs. METHUEN beg to announce that they are about to issue, in ten volumes 8vo, an authorised collection of Mr. Gladstone's Speeches, the work being undertaken with his sanction and under his superintendence. Notes and Introductions will be added.

In view of the interest in the Home Rule Question, it is proposed to issue Vols. IX. and X., which will include the speeches of the last seven or eight years, immediately, and then to proceed with the earlier volumes. Volume X. is already published.

Collingwood. JOHN RUSKIN: His Life and Work. By W. G. COLLINGWOOD, M.A., late Scholar of University College, Oxford, Author of the 'Art Teaching of John Ruskin,' Editor of Mr. Ruskin's Poems. 2 *vols.* 8vo. 32s.

Also a limited edition on hand-made paper, with the Illustrations on India paper. £3, 3s. *net.*

Also a small edition on Japanese paper. £5, 5s. *net.*

This important work is written by Mr. Collingwood, who has been for some years Mr. Ruskin's private secretary, and who has had unique advantages in obtaining materials for this book from Mr. Ruskin himself and from his friends. It will contain a large amount of new matter, and of letters which have never been published, and will be, in fact, as near as is possible at present, a full and authoritative biography of Mr. Ruskin. The book will contain numerous portraits of Mr. Ruskin, including a coloured one from a water-colour portait by himself, and also 13 sketches, never before published, by Mr. Ruskin and Mr. Arthur Severn. A bibliography will be added.

Baring Gould. THE TRAGEDY OF THE CAESARS: The Emperors of the Julian and Claudian Lines. With numerous Illustrations from Busts, Gems, Cameos, etc. By S. BARING GOULD, Author of 'Mehalah,' etc. 2 *vols. Royal 8vo.* 30s.

This book is the only one in English which deals with the personal history of the Caesars, and Mr. Baring Gould has found a subject which, for picturesque detail and sombre interest, is not rivalled by any work of fiction. The volumes are copiously illustrated.

Baring Gould. SURVIVALS AND SUPERSTITIONS. With Illustrations. By S. BARING GOULD. *Crown 8vo.* 7s. 6d.

A book on such subjects as Foundations, Gables, Holes, Gallows, Raising the Hat, Old Ballads, etc. etc. It traces in a most interesting manner their origin and history.

Perrens. THE HISTORY OF FLORENCE FROM THE TIME OF THE MEDICIS TO THE FALL OF THE REPUBLIC. By F. T. PERRENS. Translated by HANNAH LYNCH. In three volumes. Vol. I. *8vo.* 12s. 6d.

This is a translation from the French of the best history of Florence in existence. This volume covers a period of profound interest—political and literary—and is written with great vivacity.

Henley & Whibley. A BOOK OF ENGLISH PROSE. Collected by W. E. HENLEY and CHARLES WHIBLEY. *Crown 8vo.* 6s.

Also small limited editions on Dutch and Japanese paper. 21s. and 42s.

A companion book to Mr. Henley's well-known *Lyra Heroica*.

"Q." GREEN BAYS: A Book of Verses. By "Q.," Author of 'Dead Man's Rock' &c. *Fcap. 8vo.* 3s. 6d.

Also a limited edition on large Dutch paper.

A small volume of Oxford Verses by the well-known author of 'I Saw Three Ships,' etc.

Wells. OXFORD AND OXFORD LIFE. By Members of the University. Edited by J. WELLS, M.A., Fellow and Tutor of Wadham College. *Crown 8vo.* 3s. 6d.

This work will be of great interest and value to all who are in any way connected with the University. It will contain an account of life at Oxford—intellectual, social, and religious—a careful estimate of necessary expenses, a review of recent changes, a statement of the present position of the University, and chapters on Women's Education, aids to study, and University Extension.

Driver. SERMONS ON SUBJECTS CONNECTED WITH THE OLD TESTAMENT. By S. R. DRIVER, D.D., Canon of Christ Church, Regius Professor of Hebrew in the University of Oxford. *Crown 8vo.* 6s.

An important volume of sermons on Old Testament Criticism preached before the University by the author of 'An Introduction to the Literature of the Old Testament.'

Prior. CAMBRIDGE SERMONS. Edited by C. H. PRIOR, M.A., Fellow and Tutor of Pembroke College. *Crown 8vo.* 6s.

A volume of sermons preached before the University of Cambridge by various preachers, including the Archbishop of Canterbury and Bishop Westcott.

Kaufmann. CHARLES KINGSLEY. By M. KAUFMANN, M.A. *Crown 8vo.* 5s.

A biography of Kingsley, especially dealing with his achievements in social reform.

Lock. THE LIFE OF JOHN KEBLE. By WALTER LOCK, M.A., Fellow of Magdalen College, Oxford. With Portrait. *Crown 8vo.* 5s.

Hutton. CARDINAL MANNING: A Biography. By A. W. HUTTON, M.A. With Portrait. *New and Cheaper Edition. Crown 8vo.* 2s. 6d.

Sells. THE MECHANICS OF DAILY LIFE. By V. P. SELLS, M.A. Illustrated. *Crown 8vo.* 2s. 6d.

Kimmins. THE CHEMISTRY OF LIFE AND HEALTH. By C. W. KIMMINS, Downing College, Cambridge. Illustrated. *Crown 8vo.* 2s. 6d.

Potter. AGRICULTURAL BOTANY. By M. C. POTTER, Lecturer at Newcastle College of Science. Illustrated. *Crown 8vo.* 2s. 6d.

The above are new volumes of the "University Extension Series."

Cox. LAND NATIONALISATION. By HAROLD COX, M.A. *Crown 8vo.* 2s. 6d.

Hadfield & Gibbins. A SHORTER WORKING DAY. By R. A. HADFIELD and H. de B. GIBBINS, M.A. *Crown 8vo.* 2s. 6d.

The above are new volumes of "Social Questions of To-day" Series.

FICTION.

Norris. HIS GRACE. By W. E. NORRIS, Author of 'Mdle. de Mersac,' 'Marcia,' etc. *Crown 8vo.* 2 vols. 21s.

Pryce. TIME AND THE WOMAN. By RICHARD PRYCE, Author of 'Miss Maxwell's Affections,' 'The Quiet Mrs. Fleming,' etc. *Crown 8vo.* 2 vols. 21s.

Parker. PIERRE AND HIS PEOPLE. By GILBERT PARKER. *Crown 8vo. Buckram.* 6s.

Marriott Watson. DIOGENES OF LONDON and other Sketches. By H. B. MARRIOTT WATSON, Author of 'The Web of the Spider.' *Crown 8vo. Buckram.* 6s.

Baring Gould. IN THE ROAR OF THE SEA. By S. BARING GOULD, Author of 'Mehalah,' 'Urith,' etc. Cheaper edition. *Crown 8vo.* 6s.

Clark Russell. MY DANISH SWEETHEART. By W. CLARK RUSSELL, Author of 'The Wreck of the Grosvenor,' 'A Marriage at Sea,' etc. With 6 Illustrations by W. H. OVEREND. *Crown 8vo.* 6s.

Mabel Robinson. HOVENDEN, V. C. By F. MABEL ROBINSON, Author of 'Disenchantment,' etc. Cheaper Edition. *Crown 8vo.* 3s. 6d.

Meade. OUT OF THE FASHION. By L. T. MEADE, Author of 'A Girl of the People,' etc. With 6 Illustrations by W. PAGET. *Crown 8vo.* 6s.

Cuthell. ONLY A GUARDROOM DOG. By Mrs. CUTHELL. With 16 Illustrations by W. PARKINSON. *Square Crown 8vo.* 6s.

Collingwood. THE DOCTOR OF THE JULIET. By HARRY COLLINGWOOD, Author of 'The Pirate Island,' etc. Illustrated by GORDON BROWNE. *Crown 8vo.* 6s.

Bliss. A MODERN ROMANCE. By LAURENCE BLISS. *Crown 8vo. Buckram.* 3s. 6d. *Paper.* 2s. 6d.

CHEAPER EDITIONS.

Baring Gould. OLD COUNTRY LIFE. By S. BARING GOULD, Author of 'Mehalah,' etc. With 67 Illustrations. *Crown 8vo.* 6s.

Clark. THE COLLEGES OF OXFORD. Edited by A. CLARK, M.A., Fellow and Tutor of Lincoln College. *8vo.* 12s. 6d.

Russell. THE LIFE OF ADMIRAL LORD COLLINGWOOD. By W. CLARK RUSSELL, Author of 'The Wreck of the Grosvenor.' With Illustrations by F. BRANGWYN. *8vo.* 10s. 6d.

Author of 'Mdle. Mori.' THE SECRET OF MADAME DE Monluc. By the Author of 'The Atelier du Lys,' 'Mdle. Mori.' *Crown 8vo.* 3s. 6d.

'An exquisite literary cameo.'—*World.*

MESSRS. METHUEN'S LIST

New and Recent Books.

Poetry

Rudyard Kipling. BARRACK-ROOM BALLADS; And Other Verses. By RUDYARD KIPLING. *Fourth Edition. Crown 8vo. 6s.*

'Mr. Kipling's verse is strong, vivid, full of character. . . . Unmistakable genius rings in every line.'—*Times*.

'The disreputable lingo of Cockayne is henceforth justified before the world; for a man of genius has taken it in hand, and has shown, beyond all cavilling, that in its way it also is a medium for literature. You are grateful, and you say to yourself, half in envy and half in admiration: "Here is a *book*; here, or one is a Dutchman, is one of the books of the year."'—*National Observer*.

'"Barrack-Room Ballads" contains some of the best work that Mr. Kipling has ever done, which is saying a good deal. "Fuzzy-Wuzzy," "Gunga Din," and "Tommy," are, in our opinion, altogether superior to anything of the kind that English literature has hitherto produced.'—*Athenæum*.

'These ballads are as wonderful in their descriptive power as they are vigorous in their dramatic force. There are few ballads in the English language more stirring than "The Ballad of East and West," worthy to stand by the Border ballads of Scott.'—*Spectator*.

'The ballads teem with imagination, they palpitate with emotion. We read them with laughter and tears; the metres throb in our pulses, the cunningly ordered words tingle with life; and if this be not poetry, what is?'—*Pall Mall Gazette*.

Ibsen. BRAND. A Drama by HENRIK IBSEN. Translated by WILLIAM WILSON. *Crown 8vo. 5s.*

'The greatest world-poem of the nineteenth century next to "Faust." "Brand" will have an astonishing interest for Englishmen. It is in the same set with "Agamemnon," with "Lear," with the literature that we now instinctively regard as high and holy.'—*Daily Chronicle*.

Henley. LYRA HEROICA: An Anthology selected from the best English Verse of the 16th, 17th, 18th, and 19th Centuries. By WILLIAM ERNEST HENLEY, Author of 'A Book of Verse,' 'Views and Reviews,' etc. *Crown 8vo. Stamped gilt buckram, gilt top, edges uncut. 6s.*

'Mr. Henley has brought to the task of selection an instinct alike for poetry and for chivalry which seems to us quite wonderfully, and even unerringly, right.'—*Guardian*.

Tomson. A SUMMER NIGHT, AND OTHER POEMS. By GRAHAM R. TOMSON. With Frontispiece by A. TOMSON. *Fcap. 8vo. 3s. 6d.*

Also an edition on handmade paper, limited to 50 copies. *Large crown 8vo. 10s. 6d. net.*

'Mrs. Tomson holds perhaps the very highest rank among poetesses of English birth. This selection will help her reputation.'—*Black and White*.

Langbridge. A CRACKED FIDDLE. Being Selections from the Poems of FREDERIC LANGBRIDGE. With Portrait. *Crown 8vo.* 5*s.*

Langbridge. BALLADS OF THE BRAVE: Poems of Chivalry, Enterprise, Courage, and Constancy, from the Earliest Times to the Present Day. Edited, with Notes, by Rev. F. LANGBRIDGE. *Crown 8vo.*

Presentation Edition, 3*s.* 6*d.* School Edition, 2*s.* 6*d.*

'A very happy conception happily carried out. These "Ballads of the Brave" are intended to suit the real tastes of boys, and will suit the taste of the great majority.'—*Spectator.* 'The book is full of splendid things.'—*World.*

History and Biography

Gladstone. THE SPEECHES AND PUBLIC ADDRESSES OF THE RT. HON. W. E. GLADSTONE, M.P. With Notes and Introductions. Edited by A. W. HUTTON, M.A. (Librarian of the Gladstone Library), and H. J. COHEN, M.A. With Portraits. *8vo. Vol. X.* 12*s.* 6*d.*

Russell. THE LIFE OF ADMIRAL LORD COLLINGWOOD. By W. CLARK RUSSELL, Author of 'The Wreck of the Grosvenor.' With Illustrations by F. BRANGWYN. *8vo.* 10*s.* 6*d.*

'A really good book.'—*Saturday Review.*
'A most excellent and wholesome book, which we should like to see in the hands of every boy in the country.'—*St. James's Gazette.*

Clark. THE COLLEGES OF OXFORD: Their History and their Traditions. By Members of the University. Edited by A. CLARK, M.A., Fellow and Tutor of Lincoln College. *8vo.* 12*s.* 6*d.*

'Whether the reader approaches the book as a patriotic member of a college, as an antiquary, or as a student of the organic growth of college foundation, it will amply reward his attention.'—*Times.*
'A delightful book, learned and lively.'—*Academy.*
'A work which will certainly be appealed to for many years as the standard book on the Colleges of Oxford.'—*Athenæum.*

Hulton. RIXAE OXONIENSES: An Account of the Battles of the Nations, The Struggle between Town and Gown, etc. By S. F. HULTON, M.A. *Crown 8vo.* 5*s.*

James. CURIOSITIES OF CHRISTIAN HISTORY PRIOR TO THE REFORMATION. By CROAKE JAMES, Author of 'Curiosities of Law and Lawyers.' *Crown 8vo.* 7*s.* 6*d.*

Clifford. THE DESCENT OF CHARLOTTE COMPTON (BARONESS FERRERS DE CHARTLEY). By her Great-Granddaughter, ISABELLA G. C. CLIFFORD. *Small 4to.* 10s. 6d. *net.*

General Literature

Bowden. THE IMITATION OF BUDDHA: Being Quotations from Buddhist Literature for each Day in the Year. Compiled by E. M. BOWDEN. With Preface by Sir EDWIN ARNOLD. *Second Edition.* 16mo. 2s. 6d.

Ditchfield. OUR ENGLISH VILLAGES: Their Story and their Antiquities. By P. H. DITCHFIELD, M.A., F.R.H.S., Rector of Barkham, Berks. *Post 8vo.* 2s. 6d. Illustrated.

'An extremely amusing and interesting little book, which should find a place in every parochial library.'—*Guardian.*

Ditchfield. OLD ENGLISH SPORTS. By P. H. DITCHFIELD, M.A. *Crown 8vo.* 2s. 6d. Illustrated.

'A charming account of old English Sports.'—*Morning Post.*

Burne. PARSON AND PEASANT: Chapters of their Natural History. By J. B. BURNE, M.A., Rector of Wasing. *Crown 8vo.* 5s.

'"Parson and Peasant" is a book not only to be interested in, but to learn something from—a book which may prove a help to many a clergyman, and broaden the hearts and ripen the charity of laymen."—*Derby Mercury.*

Massee. A MONOGRAPH OF THE MYXOGASTRES. By G. MASSEE. *8vo.* 18s. *net.*

Cunningham. THE PATH TOWARDS KNOWLEDGE: Essays on Questions of the Day. By W. CUNNINGHAM, D.D., Fellow of Trinity College, Cambridge, Professor of Economics at King's College, London. *Crown 8vo.* 4s. 6d.

Essays on Marriage and Population, Socialism, Money, Education, Positivism, etc.

Anderson Graham. NATURE IN BOOKS: Studies in Literary Biography. By P. ANDERSON GRAHAM. *Crown 8vo.* 6s.

The chapters are entitled: I. 'The Magic of the Fields' (Jefferies). II. 'Art and Nature' (Tennyson). III. 'The Doctrine of Idleness' (Thoreau). IV. 'The Romance of Life' (Scott). V. 'The Poetry of Toil' (Burns). VI. 'The Divinity of Nature' (Wordsworth).

Works by S. Baring Gould.
Author of 'Mehalah,' etc.

OLD COUNTRY LIFE. With Sixty-seven Illustrations by W. PARKINSON, F. D. BEDFORD, and F. MASEY. *Large Crown 8vo, cloth super extra, top edge gilt*, 10s. 6d. *Fourth and Cheaper Edition.* 6s. [*Ready.*

'"Old Country Life," as healthy wholesome reading, full of breezy life and movement, full of quaint stories vigorously told, will not be excelled by any book to be published throughout the year. Sound, hearty, and English to the core.'—*World.*

HISTORIC ODDITIES AND STRANGE EVENTS. *Third Edition, Crown 8vo.* 6s.

'A collection of exciting and entertaining chapters. The whole volume is delightful reading.'—*Times.*

FREAKS OF FANATICISM. (First published as Historic Oddities, Second Series.) *Third Edition. Crown 8vo.* 6s.

'Mr. Baring Gould has a keen eye for colour and effect, and the subjects he has chosen give ample scope to his descriptive and analytic faculties. A perfectly fascinating book.—*Scottish Leader.*

SONGS OF THE WEST: Traditional Ballads and Songs of the West of England, with their Traditional Melodies. Collected by S. BARING GOULD, M.A., and H. FLEETWOOD SHEPPARD, M.A. Arranged for Voice and Piano. In 4 Parts (containing 25 Songs each), *Parts I., II., III.*, 3s. each. *Part IV.*, 5s. *In one Vol., roan,* 15s.

'A rich and varied collection of humour, pathos, grace, and poetic fancy.'—*Saturday Review.*

YORKSHIRE ODDITIES AND STRANGE EVENTS. *Fourth Edition. Crown 8vo.* 6s.

SURVIVALS AND SUPERSTITIONS. *Crown 8vo.* Illustrated. [*In the press.*

JACQUETTA, and other Stories. *Crown 8vo.* 3s. 6d. *Boards*, 2s.

ARMINELL: A Social Romance. *New Edition. Crown 8vo.* 3s. 6d. *Boards*, 2s.

'To say that a book is by the author of "Mehalah" is to imply that it contains a story cast on strong lines, containing dramatic possibilities, vivid and sympathetic descriptions of Nature, and a wealth of ingenious imagery. All these expectations are justified by "Arminell."'—*Speaker.*

URITH: A Story of Dartmoor. *Third Edition. Crown 8vo.* 3s. 6d.
'The author is at his best.'—*Times.*
'He has nearly reached the high water-mark of "Mehalah."'—*National Observer.*

MARGERY OF QUETHER, and other Stories. *Crown 8vo.* 3s. 6d.

IN THE ROAR OF THE SEA: A Tale of the Cornish Coast. *New Edition.* 6s.

Fiction

Author of 'Indian Idylls.' IN TENT AND BUNGALOW: Stories of Indian Sport and Society. By the Author of 'Indian Idylls.' *Crown 8vo.* 3s. 6d.

Fenn. A DOUBLE KNOT. By G. MANVILLE FENN, Author of 'The Vicar's People,' etc. *Crown 8vo.* 3s. 6d.

Pryce. THE QUIET MRS. FLEMING. By RICHARD PRYCE, Author of 'Miss Maxwell's Affections,' etc. *Crown 8vo.* 3s. 6d. *Picture Boards,* 2s.

Gray. ELSA. A Novel. By E. M'QUEEN GRAY. *Crown 8vo.* 6s.
'A charming novel. The characters are not only powerful sketches, but minutely and carefully finished portraits.'—*Guardian.*

Gray. MY STEWARDSHIP. By E. M'QUEEN GRAY. *Crown 8vo.* 3s. 6d.

Cobban. A REVEREND GENTLEMAN. By J. MACLAREN COBBAN, Author of 'Master of his Fate,' etc. *Crown 8vo.* 4s. 6d.
'The best work Mr. Cobban has yet achieved. The Rev. W. Merrydew is a brilliant creation.'—*National Observer.*
'One of the subtlest studies of character outside Meredith.'—*Star.*

Lyall. DERRICK VAUGHAN, NOVELIST. By EDNA LYALL, Author of 'Donovan.' *Crown 8vo.* 31st Thousand. 3s. 6d.; *paper,* 1s.

Linton. THE TRUE HISTORY OF JOSHUA DAVIDSON, Christian and Communist. By E. LYNN LINTON. Eleventh and Cheaper Edition. *Post 8vo.* 1s.

Grey. THE STORY OF CHRIS. By ROWLAND GREY, Author of 'Lindenblumen,' etc. *Crown 8vo.* 5s.

Dicker. A CAVALIER'S LADYE. By CONSTANCE DICKER. *With Illustrations. Crown 8vo.* 3s. 6d.

MESSRS. METHUEN'S LIST

Dickinson. A VICAR'S WIFE. By EVELYN DICKINSON.
Crown 8vo. 6s.

Prowse. THE POISON OF ASPS. By R. ORTON PROWSE.
Crown 8vo. 6s.

Taylor. THE KING'S FAVOURITE. By UNA TAYLOR.
Crown 8vo. 6s.

Novel Series

MESSRS. METHUEN will issue from time to time a Series of copyright Novels, by well-known Authors, handsomely bound, at the above popular price of three shillings and sixpence. The first volumes (ready) are:— **3/6**

1. THE PLAN OF CAMPAIGN. By F. MABEL ROBINSON.
2. JACQUETTA. By S. BARING GOULD, Author of 'Mehalah,' etc.
3. MY LAND OF BEULAH. By Mrs. LEITH ADAMS (Mrs. De Courcy Laffan).
4. ELI'S CHILDREN. By G. MANVILLE FENN.
5. ARMINELL: A Social Romance. By S. BARING GOULD, Author of 'Mehalah,' etc.
6. DERRICK VAUGHAN, NOVELIST. With Portrait of Author. By EDNA LYALL, Author of 'Donovan,' etc.
7. DISENCHANTMENT. By F. MABEL ROBINSON.
8. DISARMED. By M. BETHAM EDWARDS.
9. JACK'S FATHER. By W. E. NORRIS.
10. MARGERY OF QUETHER. By S. BARING GOULD.
11. A LOST ILLUSION. By LESLIE KEITH.
12. A MARRIAGE AT SEA. By W. CLARK RUSSELL.
13. MR. BUTLER'S WARD. By F. MABEL ROBINSON.
14. URITH. By S. BARING GOULD.
15. HOVENDEN, V.C. By F. MABEL ROBINSON.

Other Volumes will be announced in due course.

NEW TWO-SHILLING EDITIONS
Crown 8vo, Ornamental Boards.

2/-

ARMINELL. By the Author of 'Mehalah.'
ELI'S CHILDREN. By G. MANVILLE FENN.
DISENCHANTMENT. By F. MABEL ROBINSON.
THE PLAN OF CAMPAIGN. By F. MABEL ROBINSON.
JACQUETTA. By the Author of 'Mehalah.'

Picture Boards.

A DOUBLE KNOT. By G. MANVILLE FENN.
THE QUIET MRS. FLEMING. By RICHARD PRYCE.
JACK'S FATHER. By W. E. NORRIS.
A LOST ILLUSION. By LESLIE KEITH.

Books for Boys and Girls

Walford. A PINCH OF EXPERIENCE. By L. B. WALFORD, Author of 'Mr. Smith.' With Illustrations by GORDON BROWNE. *Crown 8vo.* 6s.

'The clever authoress steers clear of namby-pamby, and invests her moral with a fresh and striking dress. There is terseness and vivacity of style, and the illustrations are admirable.'—*Anti-Jacobin.*

Molesworth. THE RED GRANGE. By Mrs. MOLESWORTH, Author of 'Carrots.' With Illustrations by GORDON BROWNE. *Crown 8vo.* 6s.

'A volume in which girls will delight, and beautifully illustrated.'—*Pall Mall Gazette.*

Clark Russell. MASTER ROCKAFELLAR'S VOYAGE. By W. CLARK RUSSELL, Author of 'The Wreck of the Grosvenor,' etc. Illustrated by GORDON BROWNE. *Crown 8vo.* 3s. 6d.

'Mr. Clark Russell's story of "Master Rockafellar's Voyage" will be among the favourites of the Christmas books. There is a rattle and "go" all through it, and its illustrations are charming in themselves, and very much above the average in the way in which they are produced.—*Guardian.*

Author of 'Mdle. Mori.' THE SECRET OF MADAME DE Monluc. By the Author of 'The Atelier du Lys,' 'Mdle. Mori.' *Crown 8vo.* 3s. 6d.

'An exquisite literary cameo.'—*World.*

Manville Fenn. SYD BELTON : Or, The Boy who would not go to Sea. By G. MANVILLE FENN, Author of 'In the King's Name,' etc. Illustrated by GORDON BROWNE. *Crown 8vo.* 3s. 6d.

'Who among the young story-reading public will not rejoice at the sight of the old combination, so often proved admirable—a story by Manville Fenn, illustrated by Gordon Browne! The story, too, is one of the good old sort, full of life and vigour, breeziness and fun. —*Journal of Education.*

Parr. DUMPS. By Mrs. PARR, Author of 'Adam and Eve,' 'Dorothy Fox,' etc. Illustrated by W. PARKINSON. *Crown 8vo.* 3s. 6d.

'One of the prettiest stories which even this clever writer has given the world for a long time.'—*World.*

Meade. A GIRL OF THE PEOPLE. By L. T. MEADE, Author of 'Scamp and I,' etc. Illustrated by R. BARNES. *Crown 8vo.* 3s. 6d.

'An excellent story. Vivid portraiture of character, and broad and wholesome lessons about life.'—*Spectator.*

'One of Mrs. Meade's most fascinating books.'—*Daily News.*

Meade. HEPSY GIPSY. By L. T. MEADE. Illustrated by EVERARD HOPKINS. *Crown 8vo, 2s. 6d.*

'Mrs. Meade has not often done better work than this.'—*Spectator.*

Meade. THE HONOURABLE MISS : A Tale of a Country Town. By L. T. MEADE, Author of 'Scamp and I,' 'A Girl of the People,' etc. With Illustrations by EVERARD HOPKINS. *Crown 8vo, 3s. 6d.*

Adams. MY LAND OF BEULAH. By MRS. LEITH ADAMS. With a Frontispiece by GORDON BROWNE. *Crown 8vo, 3s. 6d.*

English Leaders of Religion

Edited by A. M. M. STEDMAN, M.A. *With Portrait, crown 8vo, 2s. 6d.*

A series of short biographies, free from party bias, of the most prominent leaders of religious life and thought in this and the last century.

2/6

The following are already arranged—

CARDINAL NEWMAN. By R. H. HUTTON. [*Ready.*

'Few who read this book will fail to be struck by the wonderful insight it displays into the nature of the Cardinal's genius and the spirit of his life.'—WILFRID WARD, in the *Tablet.*

'Full of knowledge, excellent in method, and intelligent in criticism. We regard it as wholly admirable.'—*Academy.*

JOHN WESLEY. By J. H. OVERTON, M.A. [*Ready.*
'It is well done: the story is clearly told, proportion is duly observed, and there is no lack either of discrimination or of sympathy.'—*Manchester Guardian.*

BISHOP WILBERFORCE. By G. W. DANIEL, M.A. [*Ready.*
CHARLES SIMEON. By H. C. G. MOULE, M.A. [*Ready.*
JOHN KEBLE. By W. LOCK, M.A. [*Nov.*
F. D. MAURICE. By COLONEL F. MAURICE, R.E.
THOMAS CHALMERS. By Mrs. OLIPHANT.
CARDINAL MANNING. By A. W. HUTTON, M.A. [*Ready.*

Other volumes will be announced in due course.

University Extension Series

A series of books on historical, literary, and scientific subjects, suitable for extension students and home reading circles. Each volume will be complete in itself, and the subjects will be treated by competent writers in a broad and philosophic spirit.

Edited by J. E. SYMES, M.A.,
Principal of University College, Nottingham.

Crown 8vo. 2s. 6d.

2/6

The following volumes are ready:—

THE INDUSTRIAL HISTORY OF ENGLAND. By H. DE B. GIBBINS, M.A., late Scholar of Wadham College, Oxon., Cobden Prizeman. *Second Edition.* With Maps and Plans. [*Ready.*
'A compact and clear story of our industrial development. A study of this concise but luminous book cannot fail to give the reader a clear insight into the principal phenomena of our industrial history. The editor and publishers are to be congratulated on this first volume of their venture, and we shall look with expectant interest for the succeeding volumes of the series.'—*University Extension Journal.*

A HISTORY OF ENGLISH POLITICAL ECONOMY. By L. L. PRICE, M.A., Fellow of Oriel College, Oxon.

PROBLEMS OF POVERTY: An Inquiry into the Industrial Conditions of the Poor. By J. A. HOBSON, M.A.

VICTORIAN POETS. By A. SHARP.

THE FRENCH REVOLUTION. By J. E. SYMES, M.A.

MESSRS. METHUEN'S LIST 15

PSYCHOLOGY. By F. S. GRANGER, M.A., Lecturer in Philosophy at University College, Nottingham.

THE EVOLUTION OF PLANT LIFE: Lower Forms. By G. MASSEE, Kew Gardens. With Illustrations.

AIR AND WATER. Professor V. B. LEWES, M.A. Illustrated.

THE CHEMISTRY OF LIFE AND HEALTH. By C. W. KIMMINS, M.A. Camb. Illustrated.

THE MECHANICS OF DAILY LIFE. By V. P. SELLS, M.A. Illustrated.

ENGLISH SOCIAL REFORMERS. H. DE B. GIBBINS, M.A.

ENGLISH TRADE AND FINANCE IN THE SEVENTEENTH CENTURY. By W. A. S. HEWINS, B.A.

The following volumes are in preparation :—

NAPOLEON. By E. L. S. HORSBURGH, M.A. Camb., U. E. Lecturer in History.

ENGLISH POLITICAL HISTORY. By T. J. LAWRENCE, M.A., late Fellow and Tutor of Downing College, Cambridge, U. E. Lecturer in History.

AN INTRODUCTION TO PHILOSOPHY. By J. SOLOMON, M.A. Oxon., late Lecturer in Philosophy at University College, Nottingham.

THE EARTH: An Introduction to Physiography. By E. W. SMALL, M.A.

Social Questions of To-day

Edited by H. DE B. GIBBINS, M.A.

Crown 8vo, 2s. 6d.

2/6

A series of volumes upon those topics of social, economic, and industrial interest that are at the present moment foremost in the public mind. Each volume of the series will be written by an author who is an acknowledged authority upon the subject with which he deals.

The following Volumes of the Series are ready :—

TRADE UNIONISM—NEW AND OLD. By G. HOWELL, M.P., Author of 'The Conflicts of Capital and Labour.

THE CO-OPERATIVE MOVEMENT TO-DAY. By G. J HOLYOAKE, Author of 'The History of Co-operation.'

MUTUAL THRIFT. By Rev. J. FROME WILKINSON, M.A., Author of 'The Friendly Society Movement.'

PROBLEMS OF POVERTY: An Inquiry into the Industrial Conditions of the Poor. By J. A. HOBSON, M.A.

THE COMMERCE OF NATIONS. By C. F. BASTABLE, M.A., Professor of Economics at Trinity College, Dublin.

THE ALIEN INVASION. By W. H. WILKINS, B.A., Secretary to the Society for Preventing the Immigration of Destitute Aliens.

THE RURAL EXODUS. By P. ANDERSON GRAHAM.

LAND NATIONALIZATION. By HAROLD COX, B.A.

A SHORTER WORKING DAY. By H. DE B. GIBBINS (Editor), and R. A. HADFIELD, of the Hecla Works, Sheffield.

The following Volumes are in preparation :—

ENGLISH SOCIALISM OF TO-DAY. By HUBERT BLAND one of the Authors of 'Fabian Essays.'

POVERTY AND PAUPERISM. By Rev. L. R. PHELPS, M.A., Fellow of Oriel College, Oxford.

ENGLISH LAND AND ENGLISH MEN. By Rev. C. W. STUBBS, M.A., Author of 'The Labourers and the Land.'

CHRISTIAN SOCIALISM IN ENGLAND. By Rev. J CARTER, M.A., of Pusey House, Oxford.

THE EDUCATION OF THE PEOPLE. By J. R. DIGGLE, M.A., Chairman of the London School Board.

WOMEN'S WORK. By LADY DILKE, MISS BEILLEY, and MISS ABRAHAM.

RAILWAY PROBLEMS PRESENT AND FUTURE. By R. W. BARNETT, M.A., Editor of the 'Railway Times.'

www.ingramcontent.com/pod-product-compliance
Lightning Source LLC
Chambersburg PA
CBHW020136170426
43199CB00010B/761